Candle Time

Hanukkah

Jennifer Blizin Gillis

Heinemann Library
Chicago, Illinois

Customer Service 888-454-2279
Visit our website at www.heinemannlibrary.com

Designed by Sue Emerson, Heinemann Library; Page layout by Ginkgo Creative, Inc.
Printed and bound in the U.S.A. by Lake Book

06 05 04 03 02
10 9 8 7 6 5 4 3 2 1

Library of Congress Cataloging-in-Publication Data
Gillis, Jennifer, 1950-
    Hanukkah / Jennifer Blizin Gillis.
        p. cm. — (Candle time)
Includes index.
Summary: A simple introduction to the symbols, celebration, and traditions of Hanukkah.
    ISBN 1-58810-530-X (HC), ISBN 1-58810-739-6 (Pbk.)
    1. Hanukkah—Juvenile literature. 2. Hanukkah. [1. Hanukkah. 2. Holidays.]   I. Title. II. Series.
    BM695.H3 G554 2002
    296.4'35—dc21

                    2001004645

Acknowledgments
The author and publishers are grateful to the following for permission to reproduce copyright material:
pp. 4, 8, 16 Lawrence Migdale; p. 5 Giraidon/Art Resource, NY; p. 7 Image Select/Art Resource, NY; p. 9 David R. Frazier; pp. 10, 14 Owen Franken/Corbis; p. 11 Mark Thiessen/Corbis; pp. 12, 17, 20 Michael Newman/Photo Edit Inc.; p. 13 TRIP/S. Shapiro; p. 15 Greg Smith/Index Stock Imagery; p. 18 Bill Aron/Photo Edit Inc.; p. 19 Richard T. Nowitz; p. 21 Laura Dwight/Corbis; p. 22 Shaffer-Smith/Index Stock Imagery

Cover photograph courtesy of Owen Franken/Corbis

Every effort has been made to contact copyright holders of any material reproduced in this book. Any omissions will be rectified in subsequent printings if notice is given to the publisher.

Special thanks to our advisory panel for their help in the preparation of this book:
Eileen Day, Preschool Teacher
Chicago, IL

Paula Fischer, K–1 Teacher
Indianapolis, IN

Sandra Gilbert,
Library Media Specialist
Houston, TX

Angela Leeper,
Educational Consultant
North Carolina Department
of Public Instruction
Raleigh, NC

Pam McDonald, Reading Teacher
Winter Springs, FL

Melinda Murphy,
Library Media Specialist
Houston, TX

Helen Rosenberg, MLS
Chicago, IL

Anna Marie Varakin, Reading Instructor
Western Maryland College

Special thanks also to Dr. Betsy Katz for her comments in the preparation of this book.

Some words are shown in bold, **like this.**
You can find them in the picture glossary on page 23.
You say HAHN-uh-kuh.

Contents

What Is Hanukkah?

Hanukkah is a candle time.

It is the Jewish festival of lights.

Jewish people remember a time long ago.

They won a war and took back a building called the **Temple**.

When Do People Celebrate Hanukkah?

NOVEMBER						
					1	2
3	4	5	6	7	8	9
10	11	12	13	14	15	16
17	18	19	20	21	22	23
24	25	26	27	28	29	30

DECEMBER						
1	2	3	4	5	6	7
8	9	10	11	12	13	14
15	16	17	18	19	20	21
22	23	24	25	26	27	28
29	30	31				

Each year, Hanukkah starts on a different day.

It lasts for eight days and nights in November or December.

The eight days remind Jewish people of the oil lamps in the **Temple**.

Just a little bit of oil lasted for eight days.

What Do People Do During Hanukkah?

People get together with their family and friends.

They decorate their houses.

There are special foods, songs, and games.

There may be Hanukkah parties.

What Lights Are There at Hanukkah?

menorah   shamash

People put candles in a **menorah.**

They light them with a candle called a **shamash.**

Each night, people light one more candle.

Some menorahs are electric!

What Do Hanukkah Decorations Look Like?

Hanukkah decorations can be many colors.

People make cut-out candles and **menorahs.**

The candles and menorahs can be made from paper or cloth.

What Foods Do People Eat for Hanukkah?

People eat **latkes** during Hanukkah.

They are potato pancakes cooked in oil.

People also eat Hanukkah **gelt.**

Hanukkah gelt is chocolate wrapped in gold to look like money.

How Do People Dress for Hanukkah?

Some people wear their best clothes.

Other people wear jeans and sweaters.

kippah

Some people wear a **kippah.**

A kippah is a small cap.

What Games Do People Play During Hanukkah?

Children play the **dreidel** game.

They can win candy or money.

A dreidel is a spinning top
with four sides.

Each side has a letter in
Hebrew writing.

Are There Gifts for Hanukkah?

Families and friends give each other gifts.

Some families give gifts each night of Hanukkah.

Gifts can be things people buy in
a store.

Some children make the gifts they
give their family.

Quiz

What are these Hanukkah things called?

Look for the answers on page 24.

? ? ? ?

Picture Glossary

dreidel
(DRAY-dl)
pages 18, 19

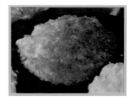
latke
(LAHT-keh)
page 14

gelt
page 15

menorah
(min-OHR-uh)
pages 10, 11,
12, 13

**Hebrew
writing**
page 19

shamash
(SHA-mash)
page 10

kippah
(KEY-pah)
page 17

Temple
pages 5, 7

23

Note to Parents and Teachers

Reading for information is an important part of a child's literacy development. Learning begins with a question about something. Help children think of themselves as investigators and researchers by encouraging their questions about the world around them. Each chapter in this book begins with a question. Read the question together. Look at the pictures. Talk about what you think the answer might be. Then read the text to find out if your predictions were correct. Think of other questions you could ask about the topic, and discuss where you might find the answers. Assist children in using the picture glossary and the index to practice new vocabulary and research skills.

Index

Answers to quiz on page 22

menorah

gifts   gelt   dreidel